Confessions of A Holy Chick

A Transparent Journey of Sexual Purity

Lady Terran Jordan

authorHOUSE®

AuthorHouse™
1663 Liberty Drive
Bloomington, IN 47403
www.authorhouse.com
Phone: 1 (800) 839-8640

Published by AuthorHouse 09/11/2018

ISBN: 978-1-5462-5759-2 (sc)
ISBN: 978-1-5462-5758-5 (e)

Library of Congress Control Number: 2018910594

Disclaimer:
I would like to thank my current living family members, relatives, ex-boyfriends, and friends portrayed in this book for allowing me to recount the events that have taken place in my life and relationships. I also recognize and acknowledge that their memories of the events described in this book, may be different from my own. The person's mentioned in this book are good people and I am grateful for each experience that I have been able to encounter. This book is not intended to hurt, defame, exhibit malicious slander or injury towards any individual family member, relative, ex-boyfriend, or friend, resulting from the publishing and marketing of Confessions Of A Holy Chick.

FOREWORD

When asked to write the foreword to this thought provoking and pellucid collection of life events, I gladly and tearfully accepted. As the mother of such a phenomenal woman, I have had the double privilege and honor to watch her develop, transform and mature into a woman of faith, perseverance, and purpose. Having witnessed the growth in her intimate fellowship with God over the years, I was able to understand the significance of the magnitude of gifts that lie within her, to astutely teach *HIS* word and gracefully draw others into fellowship; by showing them the importance of having a relationship with God. Her lifestyle is evidently mirrored by her commitment towards God, no matter the cost.

Subsequently, through her faithful obedience to the call of ministry at an early age, Lady Terran began sharing her personal journey of living a holy life of celibacy with women and teens throughout northeast North Carolina; teaching purity and abstinence classes. Later, she would further advance her kingdom assignment by forming an outreach by the name of Living Pure Ministries, which has opened up numerous platforms to touch hundreds of lives—young and old, in the most profound way.

As you read this book, you will be blessed by her transparency, honesty, and passion to share her story of self-discovery. By finally recognizing her true value and worth, she reveals the secret to overcoming the temptation to live an insecure and unproductive life. Discover why the need for accountability partners is such a necessity during your journey of purity. Learn how to embrace change and forgive others. May her testimony minister to young ladies everywhere, who feel that their only option is to live a life of promiscuity and conform to the misconception of the need to be validated, by or through sexual activities.

It is my prayer that this story will capture the attention of not only women, but even men, who desire to make the sacred vow to patiently wait on God to join them in the covenant of marriage, before engaging in sexual intercourse with their significant other. Lastly, know that in the hour that you seem tempted the most, God will ALWAYS provide a way of escape!

I invite you to now travel with her in the following pages, as she reveals how she traded her pleasure, for HIS pleasure. You won't regret it!

Senior Pastor Rachel S. Liverman
Touch Of Refuge Church, AG
South Mills, NC

ACKNOWLEDGEMENTS

I dedicate this book to every woman that has lived through the mistakes of her past, and who has grown to become the *Lady* she was always intended to be.

May you continue to know and understand the value of your worth. Your true beauty is in the character of your heart. Remember....don't tilt or remove your crown for anyone!

PREFACE

*E*very woman wants to feel and be loved. From the time that we first get a crush or play house with Ken & Barbie dolls, to imagining what it would be like on our wedding day. Then we grow up and find that life wasn't the fairytale that we read about in our favorite childhood story books. We never would have imagined that love would hurt. That is to say, we never thought that love would never be reciprocated or mistreat or abuse us. Growing up in the church, we were taught that love was patient, kind and did no wrong. When I got old enough to date or have a male friend, I definitely didn't think that I would experience heartache.

Throughout my journey in life to experience true love, I found that I needed to first truly love myself. I was in and out of relationships expecting to find what I thought was the missing part of me. It has been a narrow and uneasy road to travel these past fourteen years, but the road to self-discovery is definitely worth the while.

As you read each page to follow, I invite you to join me on a journey of purity, as I transparently share my story of becoming a holy chick!

A Day With LOVE

Written on August 2, 2014

By: Lady Terran (dedicated to GOD)

I spent my time with LOVE today, with expectation along the way.
As we walked, LOVE held my hand; a gentle touch--a sweet romance.

We made some stops along the way, I tried not to smile, but my lips turned upwards, as I pondered what to say.

I took a few peeks from the corner of my eye, my heart began to flutter. Why do I feel so shy?

LOVE surprised me with a gift, and with both hands, my sins did LOVE lift.

My guilt and insecurities, they went too, LOVE spoke these words: "I've loved you since the day my Father in heaven created you."

With each sound of words heard dear, my awe struck eyes now filled with tears.

At that moment I was glad, that LOVE showed me what I never had.

A pureness of a lover's plea, to never walk away; to never flee.

To be with me through thick and thin. To stay until my journey here ends.

To comfort, and to be my guide. Through mountains high and valleys wide.

To honor and to cherish me; upholding truth, virtue, and integrity.

My day with LOVE had much to reveal, for on one knee LOVE began to kneel.

What came next, I couldn't explain. LOVE belted a song - a melody untamed.

It echoed in my inner soul. It filled each void, it made me whole.

On this day of memory, I'll write of LOVE'S gift, of setting me free.

For all my life I was bound, up until the day my LOVE was found.

CONTENTS

"Sexual purity is not some fad that changes over time.
It is and always will be a lifestyle of honor towards
God, yourself, and your future spouse!"

– Lady Terran Jordan

CHAPTER 1

My First Love

I was never the popular girl in school. As a matter of fact, I was the quiet, shy, and goofy nerd-girl in school. I got teased a lot, but my sisters and brothers would always be there to defend me. The thought of having to get up and get dressed for school brought an utter disgust to my inner being. No one knew what it felt like to be so different. Most days were spent praying to be invisible, just so I could walk through the halls of my high school. I couldn't wait to get home, close the door and take a long nap into dreamland. That's where I went every day after school—straight to bed.

Dreamland was my escape from being a total dweeb, to being a beautiful African Princess. I'd always drift right into the sweet wonderland of being the ruler of a lush world filled with wild animals and exotic islands. Then the dream would come to a screeching halt at the sound of someone calling my name, telling me that it was time to eat dinner, came bellowing over my head. Oh, how I wish I could stay in my dream of Escape! I would just keep telling myself that I had been switched at birth and that my real parents would come to get me one day. I imagined that they would come with fine cars and beautiful robes of extraordinary African designs and fabric. That day never came.

By the end of my sophomore year, I got out of my comfort shell. I started meeting new friends and I even joined a modeling group called *Eagle Couture*. Who knew, right? My older sister was a senior and was able to hang out with the older teens. She was a part of the popular group and she also had her driver's license. Our mom noticed that I wasn't as quiet as I used to be, so she encouraged my older sister to take me with her whenever she made plans to go to the school games. That was not my sister's idea of hangin' out. I was dorky and she didn't want to have to worry about what I'd go back and tell mom. Yet still, she brought me along. Of course she had to, because mom wouldn't let her go unless I went along too.

There was one game in particular that I can recall that we went to in a nearby city. She met a guy there and they started to date. From there on out I was the third wheel when she wanted to go see him, but that wouldn't last long. I was soon introduced to a cousin of my sister's new beau. He was cute. VERY cute. The kind of cute that left you staring with your mouth open—drooling.

I had crushes before, but not like this. He made me giggle and always made my heart flutter whenever I would see him. He had this caramel skin and lips that I swore had *kiss me* written all over them. We exchanged phone numbers. The only number that I could give him was our home number, since I didn't have a pager or a cell phone at the time. I couldn't wait to hear his voice, so I'd run from the school bus down the dirt lane, to try and beat everyone inside the house first. I wasn't always successful. My youngest, older brother, ran faster. He and my older sister both hogged the phone until my mother got home from work. By that time, dinner was ready and we didn't have long to talk on the phone before bed. I'm not sure if he ever called when they were using the phone or not. I didn't tell my mother that I met a guy. Of course he was the same age as I was, but I knew she may not approve. I was considered as being one of the youngest and she was very strict when it came to me and my younger sister.

Although it took a while for him to finally call me, I felt a newness when I walked the halls at my high school. I began lifting my head high and even giggling at the thought that I met my dream guy. Soon, I started to dress like the models in my modeling club. It wasn't anything seductive, just cool enough to catch the eyes of some fellas that would not have given me the time of day before. I liked the new me. Finally.

I no longer wanted to escape the world around me. Dreamland became faint and my afterschool naps began to fade away. Then it happened. My older sister broke up with her beau. My heart broke. Not because of her break-up, but because I wouldn't get a chance to see my new found love. He didn't drive and I didn't either. All we had was the phone. A part of my spark was gone. At least we could talk to each other, right? Something in me felt torn.

For the next three years, we would barely see each other. Our conversations became more and more vague and short. It seems that he always had something to do with "his boys". But what about "his girl"? It was now my senior year. Although my sister had long since graduated, I wasn't being teased as much anymore. I still didn't have my license, but my sweetheart finally got his. When would he find the time to pick me up?

We were only an hour away from each other. I was very understanding, since he was also working at the time.

Believe it or not, I'd surprise him often by sending a bouquet of roses to his job. What I didn't know, was that it embarrassed him. He begged me to stop, so I did. I just wanted to express my deep love for him. I finally convinced him to pick me up and take me some place to eat. I ignored the fact that he didn't want to go inside the restaurant with me, so I went in and got the food and we ate in his car. Afterwards, he took me back home, because he said he was getting tired. I didn't think much of it, besides; he kissed me when he told me that he was ready to go. Who can resist that? He didn't call me for a while after that. I didn't understand why, so I sent letters in the mail to reaffirm my love for him.

To my surprise, he wrote me back. Receiving the letter meant more to me, than when he chose to call me. It showed more of an effort to write, as opposed to dialing, in my eyes. My favorite smell of his cologne covered the envelope. I couldn't wait to read it! As I read each word, my heart stopped. Could I be reading this right? He felt better if we were just friends. I didn't understand. I thought he loved me? Tears flooded my eyes and I hid in the bathroom, so no one could see me crying. The next few days would be a blur. I didn't want to do anything. Had he changed his mind about us? After getting home from school one day, I received a call from him out of the blue. I barely could utter the words: *Hello?* He just called to see if I got the letter. My mind went blank. There was an awkward silence before I let him know that I had received his letter. He knew I was hurt, so he asked how I was doing. This was my moment to either tell him off or get to the bottom of the break-up. So I did what any girl who's madly in love would do. I asked him the infamous question of *Why?* As he took a big gulp, he said that I already knew why. At this point, I'm lost. What is he trying to tell me? I figured that he didn't want to say it over the phone, so I asked him to come and pick me up, so that we could talk. He agreed. I asked my mom, who was oblivious of our break-up, let alone how long we had been in a relationship, if he could pick me up and take me to get something to eat. She felt that it was alright, as long as I was back home by curfew. She was a little more lenient, since I was about to graduate from high school.

The car horn blows and I rush out of the house. I hadn't seen him since we ate together in his car that day at the restaurant. He didn't get out of the car to greet me. I had a slight smile on my face, but he looked as if he wasn't interested. We kindly greet each other and he backs out of the driveway. We sat in silence until he pulled the car over into a busy parking lot. I can still hear the loud sound, as he put the gear into park. My heart is thumping out of my chest, by this time. He turns and begins to tell me the real reason for the break-up. I couldn't believe what I was hearing.

He felt that we were drifting apart and that he needed more in a relationship. He was tired of having to pick me up to go out. Then he finally said what I dreaded to hear. He wanted to be able to have sex with whoever he was "going out" with. He knew that I was still a virgin and believed in waiting until I was married to have sex. I had shared with him early in our relationship, how excited I was to get my purity ring. My eyes were red and filled with tears and I couldn't help but cry loudly. I believe he felt guilty, because he slowly put his arm around me, in an effort to console me.

I gathered my composure and pushed him away. I didn't know who he was–who he had become. I turned to look him in the eyes and told him that I love him. What I said next shocked both me and him. I told him that I was willing to do what I needed to do to keep the relationship. Did I just really say that? I did. Soon after, we were on our way to his house to seal the deal.

By the time I got the courage to tell him that I had changed my mind and wasn't ready, we were pulling into his driveway.

My legs were stuck. I couldn't get out of the car. He called for me to get out of the car. He had already gotten out and unlocked his front door. Motioning for me to come inside, I finally got out of the car. He let me know that his mom had gone out of town and wouldn't be back until the next day. I began crying as he led me to his bedroom. I didn't know what I was doing. I wanted to run, but I was afraid. Sitting on the edge of his bed, I looked lost. However, I played along and removed my clothes. His stare made me want to put my clothes back on. I got under the covers and closed my eyes. Tears were still falling. *Dear Lord, please help me,* I whispered.

Knowing that I was nervous, he left the room for a while. I had a chance to put my clothes back on, but I didn't. Why didn't I?

When he came back into the room, he looked down and said that I didn't have to, if I didn't want to. Deep inside I wanted to tell him that I wasn't ready and didn't want to go through with it, but I loved him so much and feared losing him again, so I told him that I wanted to. He looked up with the biggest and brightest smile and hurriedly got under the covers with me. It was the most painful experience of my life! I cried when it was all over and he……he just got up, put his clothes back on and left me in the room by myself. I soon heard the front door open and close. He actually left me in his house! Where he went, I don't know. How could I allow this to happen? He only wanted that one thing from me! I slowly got up and put my clothes back on. I heard the front door open again. It was him. He could barely look me in the eyes when he came back into the room. I turned away and ran into the bathroom. This was the worst moment that I could have ever imagined.

I felt numb, looking at myself in the mirror. Who am I? I don't know. Leaving the bathroom, I could feel shame taking a hold of me. I disappointed God. The purity ring on my left hand, suddenly became heavy. There's no way to undo, what I just did. God help me! My love then calls me to come and sit with him in his living room. I wipe the last of my tears and met him there. He didn't know what to say to me, so he grabs a photo album from the night stand and begins flipping through it. He reaches over with his arm and places it near my head and pulls me closer to him. After kissing my forehead, he starts telling me about the pictures from when he was a baby. The ticking from the clock seemed to get increasingly louder for the both of us and he decides that it's time to take me back home.

We rode back with the hum of the radio playing softly in the car. He kissed my cheek, when he dropped me off. It was as if nothing happened between the two of us. I got out trying not to act so different and hoped my mom wouldn't notice anything suspicious. I stood waving my hand, as he drove away. I had lost my virginity and was too afraid to tell anyone about it. He didn't call me that night and I regretted ever going over to his house. The next few weeks, I'd be a pawn in his hands. I still loved him. After all, he was my first love….my ONLY love.

Two weeks later he called & wrote a letter in the same week. He sounded likc his old self again. I got my honey-boo back! Yay! He wanted to take me out to eat, but I wanted to go to the movies too. He told me that he didn't have enough money, so I accepted his invitation to go get something to eat. He still didn't come to the door to get me this time, but I didn't care. I ran out to the car after the car horn sounded. It was a Saturday, so he promised that we'd spend the whole day together. We talked the whole way to his hometown and stopped to grab a burger on the way to his house. He got out of the car with me this time. I wanted us to hold hands, but he said that it was too corny. I let it slide. He hands me some money and tells me to order whatever I want. We both go into the burger place, but he starts acting stand offish. I look at him with a frown and he tells me to go ahead and order so that we can go.

I order and head back to stand next to him, but he says that he'll wait for me in his car. I start feeling a little uneasy about the outing. The cashier calls my order number and I grab my to go order and get back to see what going on with my honey-boo. He somehow gets me to forget how he was acting and we start laughing at something else. His mom was home when we got back to his place. She was so sweet. She greeted me with such a warm hug and I felt right at home. We ended up talking and looking through photo albums, while I ate and her son played video games in his room. I guess he felt comfortable enough to leave me with his mom, because it wasn't long before he said that he had to go shoot some hoops with "his boys". He could tell that I wasn't too happy about that, but he left anyway. I didn't want to be rude to his mother, so I didn't go after him. A few hours later he came back and took a shower, asking if I was ready to go. Obviously I wasn't, since we had barely spent any time together. He made a joke about it and told me that we would spend more time together soon.

This was starting to get to me. I couldn't keep letting things go. It seemed as though he really didn't love me. Of course when I mentioned something about it, he immediately got upset and made it seem that I was the one who didn't appreciate what he did for me. Was I wrong to feel that way? Was I being ungrateful? I got him to calm down and apologized for not appreciating his efforts. I couldn't understand why this relationship felt the way it did and from then on I kept everything bottled inside. It seemed to work. We didn't have any more arguments

Graduation day was coming up for the both of us and his was before mine. I tried my best to get a ride over to see him graduate, but no one was willing to drive an hour to take me. He was very upset and felt that the relationship was one sided. I didn't know what to do at this point. The thought of losing him again was unbearable. I invited him to my graduation celebration, with the condition that we could be *together*. He knew what I was referring to and that changed his mind about calling off the relationship again. This was getting to be a lot more than I expected. Were all relationships like this? Would he one day become my husband? Did he see me as his wife? I just needed everything to work out, so that one day we could say our vows to each other at the altar. He was my love…….my ONLY love.

CHAPTER 2

College Bound

*T*he school year ended on a good note. I was still with the love of my life, had secured a government job, and had a full ride with my tuition to college. I wanted to go away for college, but since everything seemed to have worked out with my job, scholarship, and love life; I stayed and attended the local university. I still didn't have my driver's license, so I took taxi cabs to work and school. It wasn't easy and it was definitely different from being in high school, but I managed.

My mother re-married and moved away, so I ended up staying with my brother-in-law and older sister, until I could get a place of my own. It wasn't long before I was in my very first apartment, but trouble was on the horizon I was informed that love was seeing another girl that worked at a video store down the road from where I lived. I was livid! He was nowhere to be found and wouldn't answer his home or cell phone. I needed answers. With disdain, I left a call asking him to call me. Later on that night he called. He had never heard me speak so angrily and denied all allegations of any foul play. I didn't believe him, so I did a little investigating of my own the next day.

I convinced one of my family members to take me to the video store. They didn't know that I was going to confront girl. She had no idea who I was when I confronted her, even though I heard about who *she* was. Things got a little heated when she called me out of my name and then tells me that the flowers I gave my love, were given to her. The conversation ended with me telling her that she could have him. I balled my eyes out crying that day. My phone rang off the hook, but I didn't answer. I knew it was him. I fell asleep with the covers over my head, in despair.

I woke up to the sound of a loud knock at my front door. It was late, who could it be? I went downstairs to see if it could be coming from someone next door. Nope, it was him. That *li@#!*. That *che@##$!* I let him stand there and knock. He can stay out there, for all I care. Soon after, my neighbor yelled to *stop all of that knocking.* Reluctantly, I let him in. He had no right to show up to my house. How dare he even think that I wanted anything to do with him! It looked like he had been crying too. His face & eyes were bloodshot red. *I couldn't bare to look in his direction. Filled with so many emotions,* I just left him standing at the front door entrance. Heh soon followed me to the kitchen. I thought to myself, why won't he just leave?! I couldn't speak and my voice was hoarse from crying hysterically all day. I had called out of work and skipped class that day. All I felt was emptiness and pain. The tears flooded my eyes once more. Where was love? Love, it seemed, didn't want me anymore. He grabbed me and I tried my best to get away, but he was stronger than me. He held me, until the strength that I had left went away. We both rocked back and forth, crying. He wouldn't let me go. I had never seen this side of him before. For a moment time stood still.

Finally, I found enough strength to pull away. I still couldn't look at him. He tried to kiss me, but I wouldn't let him. What exactly was he thinking? He finally spoke, declaring his side of the story. With rage, I asked why he was even here and asked about the other girl, again. His mouth opened & I couldn't bare his response. He must think I'm the stupidest girl on the planet! Why bother speaking at this point? I chose not to believe his words. He then starts begging me not to leave him. Tears and all. He tells me that he loves me and will never do anything to hurt me. I must be the stupidest girl on the planet, because I let him kiss me! Next thing I know, we're in my bed, making what we call "love". I had fallen for love again.

My grades were solid and I had just gotten on the dean's list at school. Things were starting to look brighter. My relationship was a little rocky, but we were hanging in there. We still didn't go out to the movies or ate together in a restaurant. His excuse was that I had my own place know, so I could cook for him and he'd bring a movie over for us to watch. It never crossed my mind where he would get the movies from. I guess love is blind. All that mattered was that I was happy and we were together. It wasn't long before rumors started to resurface. This time I didn't pay them any mind. They probably were old anyway and I had forgiven him.

A year later, during my sophomore year, he called and stated that he just wanted to be friends. I didn't understand what happened. We seemed to be doing well. I told him to leave me alone and to never call me again. Why was this happening to me? It was like a roller coaster and I wanted the ride to be over. He never tried to contact me after that. Maybe it was for the best. I ended up finally getting my driver's license and bought a car. That was the best feeling of my young adulthood. I had my own place, my own car, and an awesome job with the government. Who needed what's his face anyway?

College was pretty cool. I didn't do much outside of work and school. Going to church was my idea of having a good time. After re-dedicating my life to God, my focus came back. I started singing in the church choir again and even began teaching youth Sunday school. A friend that I met in computer class at the university was getting married and wanted me to be one of her bridesmaids. I accepted and was excited to see that real love still existed. I personally had no desire to be in another relationship. Being single was the best thing for me to experience at this point of my life. That status was short lived after I caught the eye of one of the groomsmen at the wedding rehearsal. Now he was a very tall glass of water and very handsome. No matter how many times I told him that I wasn't looking for a friend or a relationship right now, he kept pursuing me. I think that's what stuck to me the most. He had a relentless pursuit.

I wouldn't give him my number, so he figured that I would be visiting my friend's mother after the rehearsal, so he called me on her phone. Who is this guy? What does he want with me? I really don't have time for games. I took the call in another room of the house; of course I knew that everyone would be listening in the other room. We briefly chatted and he turned out to be a pretty nice guy. My guard was still up, however. He gave me his number and told me to call him when I had the time. Of course I didn't make any promises. We had another rehearsal the night before and he walked me down the aisle, without any pressure. I caught him looking at me a few times, but he kept his distance. I liked that he wasn't pushy, but I still wasn't ready for a relationship. The day of the wedding he was a bit comical, pointing out different things as we walked down the aisle. I laugh now, remembering some of the things he whispered that kept me smiling.

During the wedding banquet, I declined his offer to dance. He was embarrassed because of the way I acted in front of everyone when he asked me. He left the banquet hall and afterwards I felt bad. I apologized to my friend and she said that I should give him a chance, since he was only trying to be nice to me. My emotional guards were at an all time high. I was determined to not let anyone hurt me again. Barely eating, I sat alone at the wedding party table. When it was time to catch the bouquet, I pretended to put my arms in the air. It was a beautiful wedding and I was honored to be a part of such a special occasion. My friend was off to her honeymoon to start her new life and I would head back home.

While helping to clean up breakdown the tables and chairs, one of the bridesmaids let me know that one of the groomsmen was outside in his car waiting for me. I was glad that he came back, because I needed to apologize to him face-to-face for the way I treated him. He accepted my apology and let me know how he was hurt by actions. We called a truce and he asked me to call him to make sure that I made it home safely. I thought that was sweet. What's his face NEVER seemed to care for my safety. We developed a bond over the phone. He was quite different. He was funny. He was straight to the point. I didn't have to guess with him. He wasn't pushy or ever rude to me. It was like dreamland all over again. I hadn't visited dreamland in a long time.

I told him my stance waiting to have sex before marriage and he wasn't bothered by it all. Could this be the one? He never complained about coming to see me. In fact, he would always make plans to take me out (movies and all), whenever he'd visit. We even went to church together. He surprised me one day, by coming into a Friday night service and walking up to the altar for salvation. Earlier he had asked what my plans were that night and I told him. I invited him to the service, but he turned it down, saying that maybe he would go another time. All I could do was cry, thanking God that he would give his life to him. The preacher knew we were dating and had called me to come up to the altar with him. I hugged him and congratulated him for giving his life over to the Lord. This was truly the best Friday night service ever!

Our dating became more serious and he asked me to marry him. I was shocked and couldn't find the words to answer him. I thought he was joking at first, but he was serious. I told him that I needed some time to think about it and would give him an answer soon. He was taken aback, but respected my decision. Two days later I gave him my answer and it was YES! We both were very excited and one thing led to another. Yep. We sinned. To be sure it was okay? It was just that one time. It turned out that the onetime became many times. We just kept telling each other that we were getting married, even though we would repent afterwards. After a while I stopped singing in the choir and teaching Sunday school. The guilt was too much for me to handle, so I started skipping church. I had let God & myself down again. It seemed I visited this road all too often. We had to stop. To be sure we could wait until we were married.

I had already started planning the wedding and he even helped me pick out this fabulous dress from David's Bridal magazine.

I knew he would understand, so I called to tell him the news of us abstaining from sex, until we got married. He was hesitant at first and asked if I was cheating on him. I got angry and asked why he would think such a thing. I told him that it wasn't right in the eyes of God and that we needed to do things the right way. We didn't stay on the phone very long after that. Why was love so challenging? He still came to visit me, but didn't spend the night. I could tell that it was bothering him, but I left it alone. We would have bible study at my house and he would bring over Chinese takeout or food from one of his favorite soul food restaurants. His visits became less frequent.

I was scheduled for a dress fitting at David's Bridal that weekend and he agreed to take me. Something must have happened in between that time, because that Friday before my fitting he called me at work. I thought that was very strange. He never did that before. Feeling concerned, I ask if everything was alright. He begins breaking up with me over the phone. Are you serious? This is a government phone and he can't wait to call me when I get off from work to tell me that he just wants to be my friend. I must not have gotten the memo that day, because that caught me totally off guard. I tell him that I couldn't talk at that moment, so he said that he'd call me when I got off.

At this point, I feel like I'm on *Candid Camera* and someone is gonna come from around the corner and say *gotcha!* I finally get home from work and wait for his call. The phone rings. Should I pick up? I know that what I'm about to hear will devastate me. The guest list had already been written, the food had already been planned, the bridal party had already been notified, singers had been tentatively booked, announcement cards had been ordered, ect. I gather the strength to pick up. *Hello?* He responded as if nothing was wrong. I break the monotony of the conversation and ask why he called me at work to tell me that. He stated that he had been working the nerve to tell me and that was the only time that he was able to get the courage to do so. He still wanted to be *friends-with-benefits*, because he still loved me. The tears started flowing and I began sobbing. I couldn't stay on the phone, so I hung up.

He calls me back and tries to soothe me, but it's not working. We both hang up. Everything had become so surreal. I wanted to die. By my junior year in college I was in such a depressed state, that my grades were gravely affected by it and I lost my scholarship. Consequently, I had no appetite. I would only eat if I felt light headed, but it was only enough so that I wouldn't pass out. Why didn't *love* love me? I had come too far to drop out of school, so I took out student loans to cover my tuition for two more years, but never made it on the honors list again. I stopped going to church altogether and distanced myself from everybody else. The pain wouldn't go away and neither did the memories of what I once had. I thought I had finally found true love—a love that loved me back. Maybe it was too good to be true. Where was dreamland?

He called and left messages, but I wouldn't return them. I found myself contemplating suicide to rid myself of the pain that I felt deep down. I took a long knife from the kitchen drawer and stood over the toilet in the bathroom. I just couldn't bring myself to do it, so I threw the knife and slid down the tiled wall in anguish. *God where are you?*, I cried out! No one knew my pain. I suffered in silence. My weight loss was noticeable, but all I got were compliments. I had gained weight from being happy when I was with him, but the sadness of my broken heart melted it all away.

I started lashing out in anger with my body. I called what's his face and connected with him. I knew we would never be in a relationship. I just needed to be held, even though it wasn't really real. I met another guy at the same time and fooled around with him too. I was in way over my head and had become someone I never thought of becoming. I didn't know the woman looking back at me in the mirror anymore. I called off the fling with the random guy, but kept fooling around with what's his face.

He was familiar. He knew me. I knew him. It never took away the pain that I felt. He visited, but only at night. Then one day the flash of why our relationship never worked out came to me. He knew how to manipulate my heart. I gave him what he wanted. I used to think that if I'd just allow him to touch me here or touch me there, it'd be okay. What I found was that it seduced me long enough to turn into full fledged sexual intercourse. I just wanted to make him happy, but in turn it made me feel cheap. I knew he didn't truly love me—only the idea that he could turn a church girl. The day I woke up and started saying 'NO!' was the day I lost him, but gained my dignity and gave my everything back to God.

CHAPTER 3

Staying Pure

*I*t wasn't easy saying no. I now had to deal with the pain again, this time without any distractions. My favorite pastime is writing, so my journey began with writing. Whenever I felt pain, I wrote in a journal. I also started praying to God more. I went to the local Christian bookstore and bought self-help books and inspirational videos that would help me on my newfound journey of staying pure. It was very tempting to dial old numbers that I knew would fulfill my flesh. Eventually, I deleted them or threw them away. I was committed to my vow of celibacy.

During my time of intimate fellowship with God, there were so many layers that had to be removed. Things that I never knew were there surfaced and were removed through prayer by God himself. The root cause of the pain that I felt was actually spiritual. I learned about soul ties in the prerequisite purity class for my purity ceremony years prior, but didn't understand how detrimental they'd become in my own life. Had I not surrendered during the time that I did, the course of my life could have been a lot worse.

As each layer was removed I regained my clarity. Things had gotten so foggy before. I still had to overcome how I viewed the woman looking back at me in the mirror, but I had made major leaps and bounds with committing myself back to holiness. As I studied God's word in the bible, I felt a cleansing. The stains from my past were being wiped clean. I felt love again, but this time it was different. It wasn't tainted. It was pure. It was real. I finally fell into the arms of the only one that could hold me the right way—Jesus. My hunger grew for the knowledge of God's word like never before.

I made it to my senior year of college and after a long day of school and work, all I wanted to come home to was reading my bible. I had started writing an outline for purity. This outline was my journey of purity. I never knew that it would be the start of me teaching others of how to walk in purity. By the time I graduated college I was back teaching youth Sunday school and even started teaching purity classes. I had always loved mentoring the youth. I found my purpose and my mission was to teach teenagers the importance of living a holy lifestyle of abstinence. It started a one church and then the message grew and I began teaching at several churches within the local community and a few abroad.

I graduated with a degree in Business Administration and had started working at a local bank. I shunned the thought of being in a relationship, because I was still going through my healing process and was focusing on the ministry that God had birthed in me. Extremely active in both the church and the community, I simply didn't have the time to do anything else. I started graduate school two and half years later, which kept me pretty busy too. What I didn't factor in was that I still needed balance in my life. I didn't leave any room for me to have fun. That meant that I really didn't trust myself. Slowly, surely I began taking myself out to the movies and dinner. It was different, but I needed to learn how to love me.

I spent four years in banking and ended up making the biggest shift in my life. I decided to move to another state. This was during the time when the real estate market had taken a dive. I received an offer to spend more time with my father, who lived in Maryland at the time. I prayed about it and got a release from the Holy Spirit to move. God also revealed to me that it was a necessary move for my spiritual training. Whatever God was doing I didn't want to be disobedient. I was excited to start something fresh and meet new people. It didn't take long for me to pack. I had just bought another car and gave my college car to my younger sister. It was a sports car, so everything wouldn't be able to travel along with me during the drive up to Maryland. After labeling the boxes, I only kept the items that I would need, until I could make a second trip for the rest of my things. I put my furniture and the things that were left into a small storage unit

At the time I was renting a single wide trailer and had returned my keys to my landlord. I made arrangements to stay my youngest older brother and his wife. They lived in Virginia Beach at the time. It was only for a few days, before I left for Maryland. I wanted to make sure that I had everything squared away in North Carolina before moving. This was a big step for me. I had never really traveled that far away from home. I was open for change and I was filled with what the future might hold for me up there.

The night before I left Virginia Beach, I got a call from my father. He sadly informed me that I wouldn't be able to stay at his place after all and had spoken with one of his ex-police partners about a vacant room she wanted to rent out. I was heartbroken. We had agreed that I would stay at his place until I found a job, hopefully one that was in the federal government. I had a thousand or more in my checking account and if push came to shove, I planned on emptying my Fidelity Investment account, from my 401K plan at the bank. He was able to put me on three-way with his ex-police partner. After discussing the rent for the room, I needed some time to think things over. They both understood.

What was happening here? I had already moved all of my things, wasn't working anymore, and had no place to live. I needed to pray some more. I got the green light from God to go forward with the move. I called my father back, let him know my decision and he passed the message along to his ex-police partner. That was the longest night of my life. What was I getting myself into?

Reflecting back over the seasons of my life, I saw the pattern of loss, especially in the area of love. Was God taking me on a deeper level of self discovery? Was it connected to the relationship that I needed to develop with my father? These questions were yet to be answered, but I knew God would lead me straight towards them.

CHAPTER 4

Moving On

*M*orning was fast approaching. I spent most of the night tossing and turning after the phone call. This was the moment that would reveal my complete obedience to God, even if I didn't understand it all. Reaching for my cell phone, I glanced at the time. It was 3:00 AM. Only two more hours before I would pack the rest of my clothes and small items I had unpacked to stay with the few days with my brother and sister-in-law; and head on the road to my future. With my eyes clothes, I gently rocked myself back to sleep.

Startled by the thrilling sound of my alarm, I exhaustedly hit the snooze button. The time had come. Laying there for five more minutes, the alarm sounded and I got up to face my destiny. Kneeling to say my prayers, I could sense the difference of the soon-to-be day. It was still dark, but there was something new about it. After praying, I felt an overwhelmingly presence of peace. God knew how my night had gone, so he gave me a reassurance that all was well. Thank you God. Hurriedly, I dressed for my journey with a T-shirt, the most comfortable pair of jeans that I owned, and some tennis shoes for the long ride. My final good-bye was turned into *"see you later"*. My family didn't want to see me go, but I know they loved me and wanted what was best for me—even if it meant traveling three and a half hours away in obedience to God.

Packed and ready to go, I got in the car and headed for Maryland. There weren't a lot of cars on the road, as rush hour hadn't started yet. I was determined not to make a lot of pit stops, so I ate the snacks that my sister-in-law prepared for me along the way. At the two hour mark, I had to stop and stretch my legs and use the restroom. I decided to stop at service station near the exit ramp. Pulling up, I decided to get some more gas while I was at it. Getting out of the car felt good and I could smell the coffee aroma from the adjacent fast food restaurant. No matter how tempting it was, I stayed focused on my task at hand. I was actually pretty proud of myself at how far I had driven alone.

Getting back on the road was bit of a challenge by this time. Rush hour was in full affect. I called my father to let him know that I was running a little late. He told me to drive safely and that he'd see me when I got there. The closer I got into the DMV metropolitan area, the more I noticed that I wasn't in *Kansas* (North Carolina) anymore. So many angry drivers zipped through each lane, zooming past me. That was my cue to put my foot on the gas a little more, in order to stay with the flow. My GPS seemed silent. Glancing down at it, it appeared to working fine. This was the longest drive that I had ever driven. I somehow managed to see the light at the end of the tunnel, when I finally passed the sign that read *"Welcome to the State of Maryland"*.

I breathed a sigh of relief while pulling up to my father's home. After sitting in my car for a few moments, I called my father to let him know that I had finally arrived. It had been a few years since we last saw each other and I was a bit nervous. While watching in my rearview mirror, I noticed how he walked up to my car to greet me. His face had a gigantic grin, as he proudly displayed the infamous *Jordan gap* with his bright smile. Opening the car door was like opening a fresh can of soda pop on a sun-kissed day. I happily embrace my father and we stand there holding each other, as if it were the first time we had seen each other. All I could hear in my mind were the words *my daddy*. That was one of the most defining moments of my adult life. Every daughter needs her *daddy*, no matter how old she is.

Afterwards, he did what any well meaning parent would do. He introduced me to almost his whole neighborhood. I was kind of honored actually. Then came the time to visit where I would be staying for the time being, but first we grabbed a bite to eat at one of his favorite food spots. Knowing that I was tired from the long drive, he offered to drive his car instead. The food was absolutely dee-lish-ci-ous! When we arrived at his ex-police partner's home, it felt strange. I had only spoken with this woman over the phone, so I didn't know how she'd be in person. She actually turned out to be pretty down to earth. The room was a very standard-size one bedroom with a small closet, two dressers, a TV with cable, and a Queen-sized bed. I would share the bathroom and kitchen with her. My dad ended up lending me the money for my deposit on the room and paid the first month portion. That was it. I would come back later in my car, with my things to move in. My father stated that he'd pick me up to show me around the next day.

Unpacking my car was a bit of a workout. I only took out enough, so that my passenger and back seats were cleared. It had been a while since I had a roommate. This would definitely be an adjustment. Worn out from the events of the day, I fell soundly asleep. The following day when I awoke, I had almost forgotten where I was. I sat up, surveying the room, before remembering my transition to another state. The time read nine o'clock that morning. I must have slept through my alarm. The house was quiet and my roommate had already gone to work. I got dressed and called my father and we agreed on leaving at eleven, to give us more time to get dressed and to skip the madness of the morning traffic.

Riding in the passenger seat, while dad was driving was a seat-belt clincher. He dodged through traffic as if he was riding in his police vehicle. With amusement, he chuckled at my theatrics, as we barely grazed the rear bumper of each car that seemed to be moving to slow for him. I eventually screamed, *"I WANT TO LIVE!!"* He got the hint and slowed his speedy movements a bit. As we pulled into a long driveway, I wondered where we were headed. It was a doggone gun range! Maybe I should have given him the memo that I absolutely hate guns! After a while of convincing me to get out of the car, I gave in and went inside.

This was where he had his target practice, so he figured he would show me how to use a gun, in case I needed it. Now I'm starting to get really concerned. Was the area *that* bad? Calmingly he assured me that he only wanted me to gain the knowledge of how it worked and that he hoped that I wouldn't actually have to use it. Less convinced, I stepped back and let him speak with the trainer on staff. I let them both know how uncomfortable I was with the noise and the trainer suggested that I put on some headgear, which resembled a large headset. The weight of it was heavy, but it did the job of muffling the noise of the gun shots. Of course dad wasn't bothered at all and took the liberty of firing a few shots at a target, to show me how it's done. I couldn't stand the thought of it any longer, so I motioned to him that I wanted to leave. Disappointed, he let the trainer know that he was heading out. When we got back to the car, he apologized and let me know that he thought it was a good idea at first.

Next, we left make a stop at his job. He was an Inspector with Homeland Security at that time and his office was in Washington, DC. His office was filled with other federal officers and police K-9 units. That was my first time seeing something like that, other than the detections shows that I watched on TV. I used to love watching *In The Heat of The Night, 21 Jump Street, Matlock, Murder She Wrote, and Law & Order*. I liked trying to solve crime, so this was right up my alley. He introduced me to a few of his fellow comrades and those whom he supervised.

He was so proud that I took the leap of faith and moved to the area. Little did he know that I had prayed and if it wasn't for God's okay, I would have never moved.

There were cubicles all around and nothing looked fancy. It was actually kind of drab; pretty typical for an environment like that. When we got to his office, I saw the picture frames of all of his daughters that were displayed on the wall next to his desk. It didn't dawn on me how much he actually adored his daughters, until that moment. There were other frames on the wall showing his achievements and recognition for excellence. I inherited that trait from both maternal and paternal sides.

Time had slipped away and we had missed the lunch hour, so he answered a few emails and we headed to grab something to eat. This time we sat and ate our food. After reminiscing and chatting a bit, he took me back to my new home and called it a day. Tomorrow I would explore the city alone. This should be interested.

CHAPTER 5

Exploring The City Alone

*T*he next day I ventured into the big city by myself. My GPS became my best friend from there on out. I didn't go far, as I was taking it one step at a time. Looking through the map on the GPS, I found a few local shopping centers to visit. It seemed like a larger version of the stores in North Carolina, so it was easy to get adjusted to. I didn't have any friends, so the only person that I could visit was dad, but he was at work. I shuttered to think of stopping by his job. The traffic in DC was horrendous. Mustering up the courage to remain poised, I couldn't help but stick out like a sore thumb, as I aimlessly wandered the aisles of each store.

After about thirty minutes of window shopping, I head back to the car to see what restaurants were near. There were so many to choose from, but I had a taste for some good old southern fried fish, collard greens and macaroni and cheese. The closest was a restaurant called *Carolina Kitchen*. Off I went to get me so much needed comfort food.

It was only twenty minutes from the shopping center that I perused through earlier. The parking lot totally was packed for a weekday and so was the restaurant. The air was filled with aromas all kinds of spices and seasonings. The line was such that you barely could get in through the entrance, but I was willing to wait to see if the taste truly lived up to its name of *Carolina*. As I approached the serving line, I heard the echoes of the infamous greeting *Welcome, Welcome, Welcome* echoing throughout the room from the servers in unison. When it was my turn to order, my eyes seemingly bulged out of their sockets from the array of dishes to choose from.

They had everything a country girl could ever ask for! I kept my composure and feasted my eyes on the fish, collards, and macaroni and cheese.

The portions were hearty and if it weren't for the glass separating the food items, I probably would have drooled over all of the serving trays! Even the cornbread looked like you could slap somebody after one bite! I didn't want to overdo it with getting the delectable looking desert, so I passed on that. After paying my bill and filling my cup at the soda fountain, I found a seat at a table near one of the windows and dove in! I think the heavens opened up after my first bite. Truly God was favoring me! Maybe this is a little bit of a marketing plug, but if you're ever in Largo, MD—go get you some of the closest thing to southern comfort food there is in the DMV.

There was no more room in my belly to take another bite. I had eaten myself happy! Good thing they had already placed everything in a takeout container. Waddling out of my seat, I managed to make it back to my car.

That was the absolute best highlight of my adventure! A girl could get used this. Now where to next? While nonchalantly strumming my fingers on the dashboard and dazing out the front windshield, I came up with an idea. I would ride through the neighborhood of where I lived, to acclimate with view of each street look and practice without using my GPS. That would be a daunting challenge, plus it would spare me the agony of sitting in bumper-to-bumper rush hour traffic. Besides, I had the rest of the year to do more sight-seeing; even though I wasn't sure the length of time I'd actually be living in the area.

As I approached the street on which I now lived, I had a notion to keep going straight. The road seemed to lead to a dead-end. I turned the car around and noticed a gentleman waving at me. He looked to be in his mid forties. Responding with a gesture of the same, he walks towards my car. I politely roll down my window to see what he wanted. He must be have been the neighborhood watch, because he told me that he noticed my North Carolina license plates and figured I was lost. Smiling, I let him know that I had just moved into the neighborhood and was just getting adjusted to my surroundings. That sparked a ten minute conversation about the neighborhood, the condition of the state, and him offering me to stop my some time to *talk*. Of course I sensed him getting a little fresh, so I respectfully declined and gladly drove away. To be sure that was not what God had in mind for me in the relationship department. I was happy with being single and celibate. There was a reason that I felt drawn in that direction, though. Only time would tell.

Each street seemed to look exactly the same, but I was determined to see if I could memorize the cross sections. After a few tries, I decided to turn my GPS back on. It turns out I was so off course from the street on where I lived. I didn't know the neighborhood was no intricate. This would definitely take some time to learn. That was a clue for me to head back home to get some rest; my step-mom had planned on taking me to a temp agency in the morning, to apply for work and I needed to make sure my resume was updated.

CHAPTER 6

The Interview

*D*ad called the morning of the interview to let me know that he and my step-mom would pick me up, because the agency was located in DC. That was a relief. I wasn't sure if I was ready to take on that feat. Everything seemed to be happening so fast, but I was happy to start looking for work. Rent was due in another thirty days and was now an impending obligation, not factored into my original moving plan.

As expected, traffic congestion was heavy. Gripping the wheel and honking his horn at the stalled cars in front of him, my dad impatiently maneuvered his way through the continuing pile of cars. What else could I do, but hold on tight. With ten minutes to spare, we made it to the front of the building. Dad needed to park the car, so my step-mom and I got out and headed up the elevator corridor to the office. The waiting area smelled of peppermint, as we opened the office doors. I let the receptionist know that I was there for my interview and she pleasantly let me know that someone would be out shortly to direct me to the meeting room. The wait wasn't long. Within seconds I was greeted by a stout bearded fellow, whose baritone voice echoed the waiting area. Standing to shake his hand, I noticed how down-to-earth he was. I generally encounter interviewers who are so stiff and professional, you don't know whether they like you or want to get out of their way. This was a good sign, as I felt more relaxed.

The interviewer guided me to the meeting room and hands me a clipboard to begin filling out forms. He quietly slips out of the office while I completed them. When he returned I was finishing the last form with my signature. I handed the clipboard with the forms back to him and he sat at his desk to read them over. Surprisingly, he began the interview with talking about his family and how long he had been with the company. We shared a few laughs and then he asked me only one question, *"How soon can you start?"* Wow! That was the shortest interview that I've ever had. Of course I let him know that I could start as soon as possible. Handing me his business car, he shared that there was a client that needed help ASAP, and that I'd be perfect for the clerical position. He'd give them a call to let them know that I was interested and would call me back with the start time and address of the job assignment. I looked up and whispered, *"Thank you Jesus!"*, as I headed toward the waiting area to meet my dad and step-mom.

I'm pretty sure my father knew that I would be hired on the spot, but I still let them know the great news. They congratulated me and we headed toward the parking garage. Dad had opted to work from home that day and needed to get back, so they dropped me off at home. I only had one thing on my mind by this time and that was where I was going to eat. Getting into my car, I turn on my faithful GPS. *Where to this time?*, I wondered. *"Ah, ha!"*, I exclaimed while putting the key into the ignition. I decided to get some chicken from the *Popeye's* next to the shopping center I visited the other day.

My step-mom and I took the Metro subway train the next day. She called the night before and let me know that if would be easier to use, instead getting caught in rush hour traffic, and would show me how it worked. I had never ridden on a train before, let alone a subway train. It was a nice 30 minute walk from the house to the station. We met at the gate and she let me know that I needed a *SmartTrip* card with money added, in order to enter and exit the rail station or bus.

This was totally new to me, but I observed and listened. She moved at a fast past as we walked to board the train. It was like a madhouse, with people yelling obscenities, pushing, and screaming. Now I knew what a *rat race* looked like. I noticed that everyone either wore sneakers or carried a bag, which seemed odd to pair with professional attire. We boarded the train and barely found two free stand-alone seats. She handed me a brochure of the subway map and showed me how to look for the stops. As she spoke, I could vaguely hear the train conductor announce the following stop. I was glad that she gave me the map. After a few stops, it was time for us to exit the train. The station platform looked like the one that we just left from. Up the escalators we went, swiping our *SmartTrip* cards in order to get out. Did I mention that I was dressed in a knee-length skirt and low heels? That was my normal way of dressing, plus I wanted to look cute in the big city of Washington, DC. A few minutes of walking the streets of DC, I slowly began to regret my choice of shoes and explained why the majority at the train station wore wearing sneakers. Keeping up with the Kardashians was irrelevant in this moment. Lesson learned.

On the flip side of it all, I got to see our nation's capital for the first time since grade school. Everyone was in their own worlds, no one looked eye-to-eye, unless they were kissing or racing to be the first one to hail a taxi cab. The air smelled musky and homeless veterans filled the sidewalks, begging for loose change and food. If that wasn't a wake-up call, I don't know what was. That saddened me. *The land of the free and the home of the brave*, huh?

CHAPTER 7

Finding A Church Home

Working for the temp agency had its advantages. I had my weekends free to continue my exploration around town. There was one major thing that I began my search of and that was my new church home. Growing up, I had been primarily raised in a family ministry and I knew the importance of having a spiritual covering to be accountable to. I visited churches in Baltimore, Silver Spring, Crystal City, Falls Church; neither had what I know I needed. Spiritually speaking, I needed the substance of the word that consisted of *meat* and not *milk*. Earnestly, I prayed and asked God to give me confirmation on the direction that I needed to take.

One Sunday morning, I decided to watch one of my favorite inspirational Christian television stations, instead. While watching the different programs, there was one that caught my attention. That pastor was a short, bald looking man who expounded the word of God with such power and authority. After watching it, I immediately grabbed my pen and journal pad to write down the name and address from the announcements at the end. I would make sure to visit that church the following Sunday.

The week flew by and I was getting excited to see the weekend. Getting up early to catch the Metro train was starting to weigh on me, but I was still thankful for finding work so soon. Sunday came and I was running a little late for morning worship, making it just in time for the last praise and worship song. The sanctuary looked like a coliseum, compared to the churches that I attended back home. Each seat seemed to have been taken, in what looked like a sea of people. The ushers graciously led me to an empty seat towards the mid-section of the church. The worship was phenomenal and I wished I would have gotten there a lot sooner, so that I could have experienced more.

As the worship team exited the stage a woman, dressed gorgeously, walked towards the stage. For a moment I thought I at the wrong church. Where with the short, bald headed pastor from the TV? I decided to stay and figure it out later. What happened next changed my life forever. This woman also spoke with such authority and power. I received a breakthrough in my mind and body instantly. This was the confirmation that God was revealing to me. As she invited the congregation to the altar, I had no second thoughts that this church was my new church home. With tears streaming down my face, I headed for the altar with my hands held high in surrender. God was healing me, inside and out.

Within two years of membership I was actively volunteering in several ministry departments at the church. The main department was the children's ministry. I absolutely love children and believe that God has a special place in his heart for each of them. I attended the church's singles ministry, where I met a group of Holy Ghost filled single individuals like me. It was awesome! We hung out almost all the time, with leadership accountability of course. There was one guy that became like a little brother to me. We were close and always talked on the phone. He was so hilariously super. As time passed, I became emotionally attached and my feelings began to grow towards him. I never mentioned it, because I wasn't ready for potential heartbreak again.

Things turned for the worse in my life after a short while. I wasn't able to keep up the payments on my car with the salary from the temp agency. My search for other employment came up with dead ends. Unfortunately, I ended up without a car, but at least I could still take the metro train. Soon after my assignment with the temp agency ended and there were no available companies that needed assistance at the time. I didn't know what was happening. It was as if I was leaving in a nightmare. Reluctantly, I called my dad to let him know. He wasn't too thrilled, because I asked if he could help me with buying a cheap car—nothing fancy. A day or so passed and gave me a call back with his answer and included a lecture of being a responsible adult. I humbly and quietly listened.

I received a call for an interview a few weeks later and got a job working as an optician. I took the bus and train until dad was able to purchase a car for me. When he did, It was a two-toned minivan from an auction. My pride had flown all the way out of the window. God was definitely polishing my character. After a year as an optician, I was promoted as an assistant manager and relocated to another store further away. The role was very tasking, in that the employees and general store manager were tight like glue. I must have posed as a threat to them, because they made it very difficult for me to do my job duties. In seven months, things began to escalate to where my stress levels where at an all time high. I was in and out of the hospital and doctor's office. It was severe. I ended up reaching out to one of the elders at my church for prayer. Things got even worse. Constantly, I asked God to deliver me from all the shenanigans filled with hate and insubordinate behavior. It was too much for one person to bear. After almost a year of no resolve, continued opposition, and days filled with me crying in the employee bathroom; I was finally forced to quit. No one should have to experience the level of hatred and pestering that I endured.

I set out to find other work, but it wasn't as easy as I thought it would be. Consequently, I lost my then apartment that I had just moved into by myself. What was I thinking? I started volunteering at my church and was allowed to use the computer to apply for stable work. I stayed with different friends that I had met at church, but they were only temporary. I soon found myself homeless and eventually applying for food stamps. I still couldn't live with my father and that devastated me to my core.

CHAPTER 8

Living Homeless

*P*ointing fingers at others for the cause of my predicament was out of the question. As an adult, I had to own up to my mistakes and errors. I was too prideful to let my mother and family in North Carolina know what I was experiencing. I felt trapped inside of a dark pit. My self-esteem hit rock bottom and I put on the illusion of being alright, when truly I wasn't. Engrossing myself with volunteer work at my church, I found solace with being around the saints of God.

The scars from my past began to re-surface and immersed myself prayer and intercession. It seemed that I became an expert at hiding my emotions. No one knew the agony that was raging within me, yet still I grew closer in my relationship with God.

The second year of being homeless, I decided to enroll in a bible college course study that my church was offering. I was didn't quite know how I would pay for my books or tuition, but I took a leap of faith and enrolled anyway. I remembered how I used to give pedicures and manicures as a hobby in North Carolina, so I would let those around me know that I offered a basic service. To my surprise they accepted and I was able to make enough to go towards my tuition. The rest came from writing résumé and research papers for others who knew I had the gift of writing. Each class brought greater revelation of who God truly is. My therapy was getting into the presence of Almighty God.

There was this dark pink vinyl bag that I used to carry around with my books in it. Everyone thought I was studying all of the time, but really I didn't have any place to keep them. Some nights I would sleep in a hidden place that I would find throughout my day while walking.

When the season got too cold, I would ask a friend if I could sleep on their couch for a few days. After a while, some people started to figure that I didn't have a place to live. They'd let me stay for 90 days and some six months to a year. It was definitely taking a toll on me and I had lost so much wait from all of the walking. I didn't worry about food as much with having the food stamps, but I had did have to worry where I was going to keep my groceries. I mainly bought unrefrigerated items to keep in my bag, but I could only carry a few to balance the weight. There was a waiting list for housing, but families with children and veterans had a higher priority.

At the three year mark of my homelessness, I had experienced somewhat of a shunning from certain individuals who I thought cared for me. I was deeply wounded by this. During one instance I had been asked to leave, after coming home from a job that I had finally gotten working at a car dealership. I was in a car accident with the minivan that my father purchased for me during before losing my first apartment, so I had to find a ride. The car dealership was walking distance from where I stayed, so I didn't have to worry about catching any rides. I remember calling everywhere to see who could pick me up and also asked if I could live with them, until I could find a place of my own. It was truly embarrassing, especially because I had to use someone else's phone to make the calls. The community was gated and I couldn't leave my things out on the ground. I finally was able to get someone on the phone that was willing to pick me up and allow me to stay for a few months.

Each place that I have lived had its own set of rules. Some allowed me to have the house key, while others gave me a curfew to maintain in order to get into the house. This time I didn't have a key and I had to figure out how I was getting to work the next day. After using the computer in their home I was able to find a bus schedule that would take me to a Metro station, but I had a fifteen minute walk from the station to the dealership. I managed to scrape up a few dollars in coins that I found in my jacket to take the bus the next day. God is a keeper. I secretly cried that night. I couldn't understand why I had to go through what I was going through. Every time I seemed to get a few steps ahead, something always pushing me ten steps back.

After a month of working at the car dealership, I was able to buy a used car and get back and forth to work on my own. During the course of my stay at my temporary home, I became involved with the administrative work of my friend's non-profit organization. My heart has always been towards helping others in need, even though I was desperately in need myself. I was also approved through a program for the homeless to get an apartment and started the process of moving in. My friend's non-profit also assisted the disenfranchised and asked if I could help with one of her clients. I agreed. At the time I was still living with my friend and was still moving my things into my new place.

That living arrangement didn't last long either. There was a misunderstanding on what was expected of me, while volunteering with the organization after work. It ended with me having to care for a homeless woman and her two sons, in my new apartment. I could only allow them to stay for a few days or I would run the risk of being disqualified for the housing assistance. Having to take the woman and her sons to and from work became burdensome. I was rushing to get to work in the mornings and picking them up in the evenings. I didn't mind, I just needed some help. After several failed attempts of trying to reach out to my friend to make her aware of the situation, I had to let the young woman know that I was no longer able to allow her to live with me, but would be able to pick her and her sons up in the evenings after work. She understood and was able to find a place to stay temporarily. It broke my heart, because I knew what it was like to be asked to leave and feel like no one cares. I did my best to help her. She finally got a vehicle and I was very proud of her. We stayed in contact for some time after that. I prayed to God that he would send the right relationships in my life, because my trust had been violated at this point.

CHAPTER 9

Another Romance

*S*elling cars was something that I never saw myself doing, but I needed more money. I had transferred from the car dealership in Virginia, to one of their sister locations in Maryland. It took me almost two hours to get to work each day from Virginia. Being the cut-throat profession that I've learned car sales to be, I stuck it out and hung in there; selling lots of cars. I was even recognized for winning a few sales contests. I could see the growth. I didn't let too many people bother me. The travel became too much on my body, so I applied for a different position with a competing dealer and took the job there. It was much closer to home and I didn't have the stress of a having to meet a certain sales quota.

My first week of working there astonished me. The representatives in my department weren't anywhere near being professional and they all were in jeopardy of getting fired. It seemed like I went from the pot, right into the frying pan. One young lady ended up getting fired for drinking liquor at her desk and cursing at one of the other reps. It was a hot mess! The manager was extremely livid by their antics and continued his search finding their replacements.

Several months had passed and the manager still couldn't find anyone to fill the two positions he wanted to replace. It was down to just me and one other rep, as the other quit a few weeks after the young lady who was drinking at her desk got fired. This last rep always called in with a lame excuse for not being able to work that day. The manager would call and ask if I could come in earlier that my scheduled shift and also work overtime. I worked six days a week, seemingly every week. The money wasn't too bad, but I was getting tired of doing all of the work. Finally, the two positions were filled, but it brought more confusion.

I felt like I was on *The Young & The Restless.* The following year there were three new reps. We seemed to get along fine. One rep was a male and he started flirting with me. I was responsible for training all the new reps and he seemed to like me a lot. I dismissed him and told him that I wasn't interested, but he persisted. Soon, I found myself going out to dinner and a movie. He seemed to be a decent guy. We talked on the phone for hours after work. My smile was back and I was falling for him. I expressed in the beginning of our friendship that I believed in courtship and didn't believe in having sex before marriage. He understood and continued pursuing me.

We started courting and I was head over hills in love with this man. We prayed together, we went to church together, we did everything together. I had never experienced an office romance before. It was a secret between him and me when we were at work, we didn't want anyone sticking their nose in our relationship. His pastors would love when I came to fellowship at their church. We drove back to North Carolina together, so that he could meet my family a few times.

He finally met with my mom, and I watched how she observed him. She would later let me know her thoughts concerning him, like any loving mother would. Of course, she respected my decision and saw how happy I was being in a relationship with him.

I would soon awake from my daydream of love and fully open my eyes to what blindly kept me captivated by him. I had been wondering if he had been hiding something from me. After thinking about it for a minute, I had noticed a few changes between us, for quite a while. There are always tell-tale signs that something is awry. I don't understand why I keep letting this happen to me. Here I am again, facing that all too familiar door called fear. I was prepared to handle, whatever was behind that door.

After work one weekend, I met with someone at a nearby restaurant, just to get to the bottom of what I was feeling. I listened intently to what they had to say, as we both shared a small fry. I couldn't believe what I was hearing. I lost my appetite after that and wanted to leave. They apologized for what they shared with me, and offered to prove that the details were true. The phone call that was made, put me in a daze, as I stared into space. My ears, nor my heart could take it anymore. I began walking away with so much hurt. I sat in my car and screamed, with tears streaming uncontrollably down my face. It was evident, by that moment, there was no longer an engagement. I could not believe that this was happening to me!

I went to work numb the next day. I didn't have anything to say. I had to learn how to forgive myself for not seeking God. I had to forgive him and learn from everything that took place after the incident that year.

CHAPTER 10

Accepting Destiny

We don't always understand the reason why things happen the way that they do. I still can't figure out why I had to go through some of the things that I did. Reflecting over the years, my views on how to overcome obstacles in life have changed. It doesn't sting as much when someone hurts me. The hurt is still felt, but my skin is thicker and my reactions aren't as dramatic. I smile in the face of adversity, expecting a better and greater outcome. I hold to the belief that my story will be used for God's glory.

Now my focus is on building up other young women and teaching them their value as individuals. Oftentimes, we sacrifice who we are, just to fit the mold of other people's perception of us. In the past, that thought robbed me from being authentic. Authenticity is the purest form of self-acceptance that we all must wholeheartedly embrace. My confession is that, though I am flawed, I find great strength in finally being able to love all of who I am.

There is a greater liberty and freedom when you choose to humble yourself and live a life of transparency. My enemies weren't those who abused and degraded me. My true enemy was my inner me. The greatest victory that any of us will overcome is the conflict waging in the battlefield of our minds. I accepted my destiny of being totally free in my thought life, and it gave me the solace to conquer the fear of being less than.

My dreams and aspirations were not sabotaged; I just needed to develop a greater strategy to win. The barriers that I thought were hindrances, were actually opportunities set up for me to win. My passion to win has grown. I remain celibate after fourteen years of facing difficulties, while walking virtuously. Through it all, I believe that God knows what he is doing and my harvest will reflect the fruit of my obedience in the end.

APPENDIX

Purity Tips

Staying pure isn't the easiest thing to do in the world. As you have read in my personal real-life account of my relationships, it is very challenging and takes a lot of prayer, along with self-discipline. Through lessons learned, I've comprised a few tips that I pray will help you along your journey toward becoming and staying pure (until marriage, of course):

Tip #1: Confess

❖ If you have messed up, like so many of us have, don't be afraid to go to God and ask for his forgiveness. Trust me; God is not holding a magnifying glass over your head, hoping the sun would melt you into total damnation! No! He has an untarnished, untamed, unconditional love for you! He wants you to enjoy a life of love, joy, peace, and everything that promotes his love and adoration for you.

❖ The second, most important step in confessing your sins, is repenting. Repentance is simply having a sincere heart to turn away from behavior that contradicts holy and upright essence of Almighty God. To do this, you must completely do an about-face in the opposite direction of the thing that is tempting you to sin. I know, I know. It's not easy and I'm not going to sugar-coat that it is or will be. However, you **MUST** do this, in order to survive your journey towards purity.

Tip #2: Forgive & Accept Forgiveness

❖ This was a hard step for me to take. Holding on to the pain of who wronged me, was the justification that I used to continue feeling sorry for myself. I know it may seem strange, but that is what motivated some of my decisions to continue fornicating and being promiscuous with a random guy that I'd met. I'm not proud of my past, not by any means, but I write this today as an example of my process to forgiveness. As began to forgive others for the wrong they may have done towards me (especially my ex's), I was able to walk in freedom, from the weight of forgiveness. The weight that lifted from my inner self, caused me to live my life with a greater passion and purpose. Forgiveness is truly for your well-being. Don't get stuck in that dark place of forgiveness.

❖ In order for you to be the best version of yourself, you have to get rid of the extra baggage of unforgiveness. It consumed me, until I started having health problems. Believe me, losing sleep and crying a sea of tears won't do any good for your health or your sanity. Forgiving was the absolute best decision that I could have made (am making). It is a refiner's fire. It is one of the beginning stages during your path of purity that will enable you to grow, develop, and mature.

❖ I also had to learn how to accept forgiveness from God. I made a lot of crazy decisions and a lot of stupid mistakes. The defining moment, was when someone that ministered to me, told me about a pencil having an eraser. I didn't quite understand what they were saying at first. I had just told them something foolish that I had done. When I grasped the concept that they were conveying, a light bulb came into my head.

(Mini Activity Insert)

- ✓ Do me a favor and grab a pencil. Yes, right now! Grab a pencil! Now look at the pencil. See how it's designed? What's on the inside has the ability to create something, out of nothing. Now find a piece of paper and write down every sin, that you've ever committed (big or small).
- ✓ After you're done, no matter how big the list is…..**ERASE IT!!**

This is symbolic of how God's forgives works. Once he forgives us, we now have a clean slate. He doesn't even try to remember what we did. It's usually ourselves or others who tend to bring up or remind us of our past—even what we did in kindergarten! Aren't you glad that God has an eraser! He has the ability to make nothing, out of something! He gave the ultimate sacrifice by giving his son, as an atonement for our sins and now the blood of Jesus has become our infinite eraser! The next time you start having those little woe-is-me condemning thoughts, go and grab a pencil and start erasing!!

Tip #3: Pray……. A lot!!

- ❖ Prayer is simple. It's like have a normal conversation, but with God. He's not interested so much of what you've done, since he already knows. He simply just wants a relationship with you, so he can show you his heart. Believe or not, it was hard for me to talk with God, during the times I felt condemned. That's why it's so important to embrace becoming transparent with God. Don't hold anything back. The more that you talk with God, the easier that it will become to listen for his reply. Remember, it's a conversation, not a monologue. He wants to dialogue with you. That means he wants an even exchange of your heart expression, along with his. We may all experience hearing the voice of God in different ways. The best part is that God wants to share unique encounters with him, so that you will know the true nature of him as a creator.

❖ Not only is prayer a great way to develop in your relationship with God, it will also give you the strength of endurance during your walk of purity. In the beginning of my purity journey, I began thinking that God was punishing me for the sexual sins that had committed. As I grew to know him, I found out that what I was experiencing were the levels of growth in my cleansing process. Choosing the path of purity is a realigning of your old ways, for HIS new ways. I admit that it's painful and very uncomfortable, but the process makes you better.

❖ Developing a life of prayer also keeps you focused. There were countless days where I had to pray under my breath. Especially when I felt like picking up the phone to call a guy I know or even grabbing the keys to drive to his house. Instead of the false comfort of some random guy holding me, I learned the value of the comfort from prayer. That is the driving force that has sustained me, recharged me, and rebuilt me in my stance for purity.

Tip #4: Become Accountable

❖ Hear me loud and clear: **"YOU MUST BECOME ACCOUNTABLE FOR YOUR ACTIONS!!!"** My journey wasn't smooth when I first endeavored to commit to living pure. I had desires, urges, and moments of weakness. The only way that I was able to hold myself accountable for not following through with my provocative thoughts, was by letting someone that I could trust and confide in, know that I needed an intervention. I recognized that I didn't trust myself being alone at that moment. I'm somewhat of an introvert, when it comes to expressing my private vices. No one wants others to look at them in a bad way. I humbly had to acknowledge that I needed help.

❖ Nevertheless, I was able to develop my CORE group. This CORE is gifted with: great wisdom, counsel, and discernment. They still hold me accountable, even though I've grown over the years. When they aren't available during the times that I need an intervention, they join with me in prayer, right at that moment. Thank God they know the power of agreement, through prayer! They know just when to call, send an encouraging text message, or even a thoughtful card to keep me on track. You will **NOT** be able to persevere in your walk of purity, without surrounding yourself with individuals who will hold you accountable, when you start to stray away from your journey!

Tip #5: Be Careful of What You See & Hear

❖ I struggled with looking at loves scenes in R rated movies. The image of that scene would long linger in my mind, even at night. I stood flat-footed and made a decision to throw away every movie in my collection that had a kissing or love scene in it. I knew the temptation it would bring and living alone had it's perks and opportunities of planning a midnight fling, without anyone ever finding out about it. I didn't want to risk the integrity of my new found journey, so I took drastic measures to make sure that I stayed in line.

❖ I even got to the point of being mindful of the songs that I listened to. All I ever listened to in the beginning were gospel songs. Sure, there's nothing wrong with that, but I needed to find balance. Now, I like to listen to cool jazz, mellow tones, opera, a little bit of rhythm & blues. The balance came after the first couple of years. I suffered many years to fight against the spirit of lust, because of the memories that sexual soul ties brought through music, scents, or words.

❖ I can remember curling up in a ball in the middle of my bed, screaming at God, as I repeatedly hit my pillow out of frustration. My body went through withdrawal symptoms and I would lash out at God. I just knew he was making me pay for not waiting until I was married to have sex. Of course, later on I learned that God was not angry with me at all and he was not trying to make me suffer for my past wrongs. It was the consequence from my actions of sin that caused me to experience these painful changes in my body.

My body craved what it could not have. Although painful, I had a made up mind to follow God's designed order of intimacy, through marriage. I'm still growing as I deal with focusing my thought patterns on the things that are Godly. I'm grateful to be miles ahead of where I used to be on my journey called purity.

Tip #6: Work On Your Goals

❖ One of the most pivotal moments of your process of purity, is getting to know the real you--your authentic self. Being single enables you to learn your idiosyncrasies. The ones that you probably wouldn't recognize, if you were in a relationship. As humans, we tend to hold back our true selves, in order to impress others. It's usually not until we've been in a relationship for a few years, that we begin peeling back the layers and removing the masks we used to cover up our flaws. We often hear about a twenty-five year marriage going south, because one or both parties weren't' as transparent about who they were or what they wanted at the time of the nuptials.

❖ Work on your goals by devising a plan of action, so that you won't feel like you're mission out or feel stuck when you finally are joined with your husband or wife. The moment that you say I do, you forfeit having a single life and mindset, to having a joint or team mindset with your spouse. That's not to say that you won't be able to follow your goals, but you now must consider how you carry out the plans for your goals with the other person. Remember, it's not solely about you anymore.

❖ I've felt some type of way seeing my sisters & brothers get married and have children before me. Then I had to learn the gift that singleness offered me. I'm pretty sure that they would love to have a moment or week just to themselves, if given the opportunity. There is responsibility that comes with whatever stage you are in life, married or single. Instead of focusing on what you haven't obtained yet, relationship or family wise, focus on pursuing your goals, passions and dreams. Everything else will come in due time. It's not the end of the world. Until then, hang out with other singles who have taken the vow of purity, explore the world, and have fun! Live on purpose, with purpose, and for a purpose!

Tip #7: Take Time For Others

❖ Mentor: Surprisingly, it's very refreshing and rewarding when you take the focus off of yourself and place it on others. I've always had a heart to help others and that's why I began an outreach ministry to teach, mentor, and train young adolescents about the importance of living a pure life.

❖ Advocate: As a homeless advocate, having experienced homelessness myself, I always make sure that I find the time to talk with and listen to what each person had to say. I know first-hand how it feels to be ignored or treated differently, because of your appearance, housing or financial situation. Being kind doesn't cost anyone a dime.

❖ Volunteer: Consider becoming a volunteer for an organization or cause that you firmly believe in. The relationships that you build will build character and last a lifetime.

❖ Babysit: One of the many departments that I volunteered in at my church was the marriage ministry. I love children, so it was always a joy when I had the opportunity to do so. Some of the couples that attended the marriage sessions saw how I interacted with the children and asked if I could babysit, when they wanted a couples retreat or date night. I would happily accept!

❖ Nursing Home Visits: Older people have so much wisdom and I love glean from them. I would schedule visits to a local nursing home when I lived in North Carolina, so sing or read the bible to them. Sometimes their loved ones were able to make visits, so just being there, made their day.

CONFESSION JOURNAL:

Writing is one of the steps, during your journey of purification. It's how you can track your daily progress. Below are few questions to ask yourself, as you log your journal entries. Keep in mind that everyone's journey will be unique and making steps, big or small, will keep you one step closer towards walking in purity.

1. What have you done to achieve your personal life goals?

_____

_____

_____

_____

2. What steps have you taken to reduce sexual temptation?

_____

_____

_____

_____

3. How have the steps towards purity influenced or changed your thinking pattern?

_____

_____

_____

_____

4. Have you developed an accountability system? If so, what does it entail? Do you have consistent contact with your CORE group?

_____

_____

_____

_____

5. From the tips given in this book, list your recent activities that involves helping someone else:

_____

_____

_____

_____

Prayer of Confession:

Dear LORD,

I confess that I have committed a sexual sin. I ask that you would forgive me for giving in to lustful desires. I acknowledge that I need your help. I ask that you would remove any soul tie that would torment me and keep me from walking in your ways. Allow your Holy Spirit to guide & strengthen me, as I commit to walking the path of sexual purity. Help me to overcome the temptation to give in to fornication, by keeping my eyes and ears away from those things that cause me to sin against your word. Cleanse my mind and thoughts from provocative thoughts. Surround me with people of wisdom, discernment and integrity who will keep me accountable for my actions.

My body is the temple of your Holy Spirit and I present my body as a living sacrifice, that I may be holy and acceptable in your sight. I put my faith and hope in your timing of joining me with my spouse. I will reserve the sexual use of my body, for my spouse. I renounce any sexual pact that I may have made knowingly or unknowingly with someone else. I accept your forgiveness and know that you have washed me from the stain of sexual immorality. I have been made whole by the power of the blood of JESUS. I choose to submit your authority in the area of my sexuality and the purpose you intend for it to be used. I declare that the devil can no longer bind me to the sexual sins of my past. I have a clean slate. My sins have been erased and I have be set free!

In JESUS name, Amen!

JOURNAL ENTRY NO. _____ DATE: _____

_____

_____

_____

_____

_____

_____

JOURNAL ENTRY NO. _____ DATE: _____

_____

_____

_____

_____

_____

_____

JOURNAL ENTRY NO. _____ DATE: _____

_____

_____

_____

_____

_____

_____

_____

JOURNAL ENTRY NO. _____ DATE: _____

_____

_____

_____

_____

_____

_____

_____

JOURNAL ENTRY NO. _____ DATE: _____

_____

_____

_____

_____

_____

_____

_____

JOURNAL ENTRY NO. _____ DATE: _____

_____

_____

_____

_____

_____

_____

_____

JOURNAL ENTRY NO. _____ DATE: _____

_____
_____
_____
_____
_____
_____
_____

JOURNAL ENTRY NO. _____ DATE: _____

_____
_____
_____
_____
_____
_____
_____

JOURNAL ENTRY NO. _____ DATE: _____

_____

_____

_____

_____

_____

_____

JOURNAL ENTRY NO. _____ DATE: _____

_____

_____

_____

_____

_____

_____

JOURNAL ENTRY NO. _____ DATE: _____

_____

_____

_____

_____

_____

_____

_____

JOURNAL ENTRY NO. _____ DATE: _____

_____

_____

_____

_____

_____

_____

_____

JOURNAL ENTRY NO. _____ DATE: _____

_____

_____

_____

_____

_____

_____

JOURNAL ENTRY NO. _____ DATE: _____

_____

_____

_____

_____

_____

_____

Printed in the United States
By Bookmasters